THIS JOURNAL BELONGS TO:

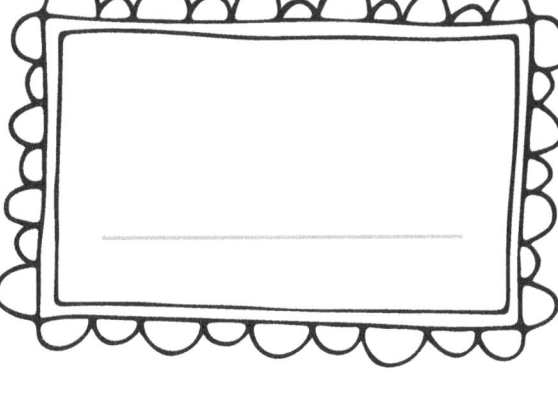

If you love our book cover, check out our design store (scan the code on the right) to see this design on a range of products including stickers, notebooks and even homewares!

scan me!

EVEN DRAGONS HAVE BLAH DAYS...

This little journal helps children identify and express feelings to encourage positivity, help manage anxiety and frustration, and generally promote wellbeing.

The deceptively simple design is based on scientifically proven methods that deliver powerful results through repetition. For example, knowing they will need to list the top three things at the end of the day encourages children to look for positive events, which develops a positive bias.

Designed to be used with minimal instruction, a daily entry should take just a few minutes to complete - we've provided an example at the start of the journal. The daily spreads are undated and can be used as frequently as desired though it is recommended to complete 5 days in a row when starting out. This journal also includes more detailed writing and drawing prompts every 5 entries to spark creativity and encourage deeper reflection.

We hope you find this journal fun and beneficial and when it's time to replace it, check out the other titles in the range by scanning the QR code below.

scan me

M T W (T) F S S

DATE: 9/9/2021

THREE THINGS I FELT TODAY:

1. Excitement
2. Happiness
3. Impatience

TODAY I MOSTLY FELT:

DRAW HOW YOU FELT ON THE DRAGON'S FACE

DID ANYTHING MAKE ME FEEL ANXIOUS, FRUSTRATED OR SAD? IF SO, WHY?

Today I didn't feel any of these things.

EXAMPLE

TOP THREE THINGS ABOUT TODAY:

1. I went to my friend's party.
2. Eating birthday cake.
3. Playing with my friends.

THREE THINGS I'M GRATEFUL FOR TODAY:

1. My mom for taking me to the party.
2. My friends.
3. Birthday cake!

DATE: _____

WHAT IS YOUR FAVOURITE THING TO DO & WHY?

_____

_____

_____

_____

_____

_____

_____

_____

_____

_____

_____

_____

_____

_____

_____

_____

M T W T F S S

DATE: _____

THREE THINGS I FELT TODAY:

1. _____
2. _____
3. _____

TODAY I MOSTLY FELT:

DRAW HOW YOU FELT ON THE DRAGON'S FACE

DID ANYTHING MAKE ME FEEL ANXIOUS, FRUSTRATED OR SAD? IF SO, WHY?

_____

_____

_____

_____

TOP THREE THINGS ABOUT TODAY:

(1) _____

(2) _____

(3) _____

THREE THINGS I'M GRATEFUL FOR TODAY:

(1) _____

(2) _____

(3) _____

M T W T F S S

DATE: _____

THREE THINGS I FELT TODAY:

1 _____
2 _____
3 _____

TODAY I MOSTLY FELT:

DRAW HOW YOU FELT ON THE DRAGON'S FACE

DID ANYTHING MAKE ME FEEL ANXIOUS, FRUSTRATED OR SAD? IF SO, WHY?

_____

_____

_____

_____

_____

TOP THREE THINGS ABOUT TODAY:

(1) _____

(2) _____

(3) _____

THREE THINGS I'M GRATEFUL FOR TODAY:

(1) _____

(2) _____

(3) _____

M T W T F S S

DATE: _____

THREE THINGS I FELT TODAY:

① _____

② _____

③ _____

TODAY I MOSTLY FELT:

DRAW HOW YOU FELT ON THE DRAGON'S FACE

DID ANYTHING MAKE ME FEEL ANXIOUS, FRUSTRATED OR SAD? IF SO, WHY?

_____

_____

_____

_____

TOP THREE THINGS ABOUT TODAY:

① _____

② _____

③ _____

THREE THINGS I'M GRATEFUL FOR TODAY:

① _____

② _____

③ _____

M T W T F S S

DATE: _____

THREE THINGS I FELT TODAY:

1. yesterday I felt ok because it was enof
2. then I felt happy because I went to
3. thustly when I came home from Muss.

TODAY I MOSTLY FELT:

DRAW HOW YOU FELT ON THE DRAGON'S FACE

DID ANYTHING MAKE ME FEEL ANXIOUS, FRUSTRATED OR SAD? IF SO, WHY?

Yesterday I didn't feel any of these things becaus it was a normil day and nothing bad happend.

miday namussid.
Athe mussid.
HI I felt oK.

TOP THREE THINGS ABOUT TODAY:

1. going to the musjid,
2. sumer shcool,
3. watching emojis.

mosque

THREE THINGS I'M GRATEFUL FOR TODAY:

1. going to summer school
2. going to the mosque
3. My Parents being nice.

M T W T F S S

DATE: _____

THREE THINGS I FELT TODAY:

1. _____
2. _____
3. _____

TODAY I MOSTLY FELT:

DRAW HOW YOU FELT ON THE DRAGON'S FACE

DID ANYTHING MAKE ME FEEL ANXIOUS, FRUSTRATED OR SAD? IF SO, WHY?

_____

_____

_____

_____

_____

TOP THREE THINGS ABOUT TODAY:

1 _____

2 _____

3 _____

THREE THINGS I'M GRATEFUL FOR TODAY:

1 _____

2 _____

3 _____

THIS IS MY WORK OF ART   DATE: _____

DATE: _____

WHAT DO YOU THINK HAPPINESS MEANS?

_____

_____

_____

_____

_____

_____

_____

_____

_____

_____

_____

_____

_____

_____

_____

_____

_____

_____

M T W T F S S

DATE: _____

THREE THINGS I FELT TODAY:

1 _____
2 _____
3 _____

TODAY I MOSTLY FELT:

DRAW HOW YOU FELT ON THE DRAGON'S FACE

DID ANYTHING MAKE ME FEEL ANXIOUS, FRUSTRATED OR SAD? IF SO, WHY?

_____

_____

_____

_____

TOP THREE THINGS ABOUT TODAY:

(1) _____

(2) _____

(3) _____

THREE THINGS I'M GRATEFUL FOR TODAY:

(1) _____

(2) _____

(3) _____

M T W T F S S

DATE: _____

THREE THINGS I FELT TODAY:

1. _____
2. _____
3. _____

TODAY I MOSTLY FELT:

DRAW HOW YOU FELT ON THE DRAGON'S FACE

DID ANYTHING MAKE ME FEEL ANXIOUS, FRUSTRATED OR SAD? IF SO, WHY?

_____

_____

_____

_____

_____

TOP THREE THINGS ABOUT TODAY:

① _____

② _____

③ _____

THREE THINGS I'M GRATEFUL FOR TODAY:

① _____

② _____

③ _____

M T W T F S S

DATE: _____

THREE THINGS I FELT TODAY:

1.
2.
3.

TODAY I MOSTLY FELT:

😃 🙂

😞 😠

😢 😬

DRAW HOW YOU FELT ON THE DRAGON'S FACE

DID ANYTHING MAKE ME FEEL ANXIOUS, FRUSTRATED OR SAD? IF SO, WHY?

_____

_____

_____

_____

TOP THREE THINGS ABOUT TODAY:

1. _____
2. _____
3. _____

THREE THINGS I'M GRATEFUL FOR TODAY:

1. _____
2. _____
3. _____

M T W T F S S

DATE: _____

THREE THINGS I FELT TODAY:

1.
2.
3.

TODAY I MOSTLY FELT:

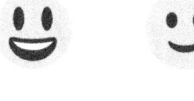

DRAW HOW YOU FELT ON THE DRAGON'S FACE

DID ANYTHING MAKE ME FEEL ANXIOUS, FRUSTRATED OR SAD? IF SO, WHY?

_____
_____
_____
_____
_____

TOP THREE THINGS ABOUT TODAY:

① _____
② _____
③ _____

THREE THINGS I'M GRATEFUL FOR TODAY:

① _____
② _____
③ _____

M T W T F S S

DATE: _____

THREE THINGS I FELT TODAY:

1. _____
2. _____
3. _____

TODAY I MOSTLY FELT:

DRAW HOW YOU FELT ON THE DRAGON'S FACE

DID ANYTHING MAKE ME FEEL ANXIOUS, FRUSTRATED OR SAD? IF SO, WHY?

_____
_____
_____
_____

TOP THREE THINGS ABOUT TODAY:

1. _____
2. _____
3. _____

THREE THINGS I'M GRATEFUL FOR TODAY:

1. _____
2. _____
3. _____

DATE: _____

IF YOU WERE GRANTED 3 WISHES WHAT WOULD THEY BE?

If I was granted 3 whishs my first one wold
be geting a gob so I can impres my perents. The wish
I woul whant the most is my famile to
have good health. I woul absloot le ask for
a money making mashen so my parents
can go on vication firt class and id help
the homles people. I mb whis come
true someday

M T W T F S S

DATE: _____

THREE THINGS I FELT TODAY:

1. _____
2. _____
3. _____

TODAY I MOSTLY FELT:

DRAW HOW YOU FELT ON THE DRAGON'S FACE

DID ANYTHING MAKE ME FEEL ANXIOUS, FRUSTRATED OR SAD? IF SO, WHY?

_____

_____

_____

_____

TOP THREE THINGS ABOUT TODAY:

(1) _____

(2) _____

(3) _____

THREE THINGS I'M GRATEFUL FOR TODAY:

(1) _____

(2) _____

(3) _____

M T W T F S S

DATE: _____

THREE THINGS I FELT TODAY:

1. _____
2. _____
3. _____

TODAY I MOSTLY FELT:

DRAW HOW YOU FELT ON THE DRAGON'S FACE

DID ANYTHING MAKE ME FEEL ANXIOUS, FRUSTRATED OR SAD? IF SO, WHY?

_____
_____
_____
_____
_____

TOP THREE THINGS ABOUT TODAY:

(1) _____
(2) _____
(3) _____

THREE THINGS I'M GRATEFUL FOR TODAY:

(1) _____
(2) _____
(3) _____

M T W T F S S

DATE: _____

THREE THINGS I FELT TODAY:

1 _____
2 _____
3 _____

TODAY I MOSTLY FELT:

DRAW HOW YOU FELT ON THE DRAGON'S FACE

DID ANYTHING MAKE ME FEEL ANXIOUS, FRUSTRATED OR SAD? IF SO, WHY?

TOP THREE THINGS ABOUT TODAY:

1.
2.
3.

THREE THINGS I'M GRATEFUL FOR TODAY:

1.
2.
3.

M T W T F S S

DATE: _____

THREE THINGS I FELT TODAY:

1 _____
2 _____
3 _____

TODAY I MOSTLY FELT:

DRAW HOW YOU FELT ON THE DRAGON'S FACE

DID ANYTHING MAKE ME FEEL ANXIOUS, FRUSTRATED OR SAD? IF SO, WHY?

_____
_____
_____
_____

TOP THREE THINGS ABOUT TODAY:

1 _____
2 _____
3 _____

THREE THINGS I'M GRATEFUL FOR TODAY:

1 _____
2 _____
3 _____

M T W T F S S

DATE: _____

THREE THINGS I FELT TODAY:

1
2
3

TODAY I MOSTLY FELT:

DRAW HOW YOU FELT ON THE DRAGON'S FACE

DID ANYTHING MAKE ME FEEL ANXIOUS, FRUSTRATED OR SAD? IF SO, WHY?

_____

_____

_____

_____

TOP THREE THINGS ABOUT TODAY:

(1) _____

(2) _____

(3) _____

THREE THINGS I'M GRATEFUL FOR TODAY:

(1) _____

(2) _____

(3) _____

THIS IS MY WORK OF ART

DATE: _____

DATE: _____

WHAT IS YOUR GREATEST TALENT?

_____
_____
_____
_____
_____
_____
_____
_____
_____
_____
_____
_____
_____
_____
_____
_____
_____
_____
_____

M T W T F S S

DATE: _____

THREE THINGS I FELT TODAY:

1. _____
2. _____
3. _____

TODAY I MOSTLY FELT:

DRAW HOW YOU FELT ON THE DRAGON'S FACE

DID ANYTHING MAKE ME FEEL ANXIOUS, FRUSTRATED OR SAD? IF SO, WHY?

TOP THREE THINGS ABOUT TODAY:

1
2
3

THREE THINGS I'M GRATEFUL FOR TODAY:

1
2
3

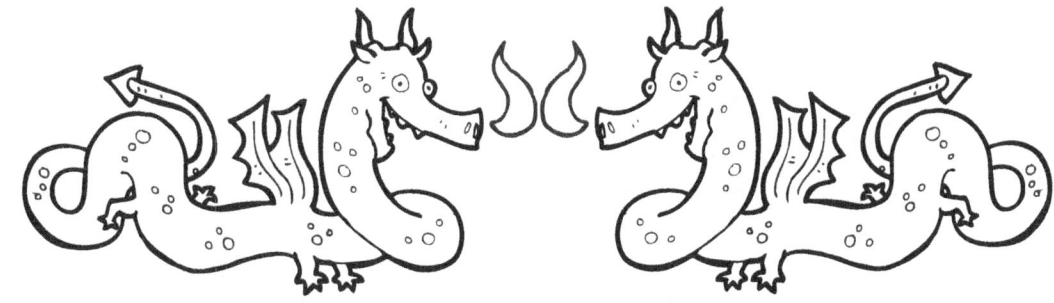

M T W T F S S

DATE: _____

THREE THINGS I FELT TODAY:

1.
2.
3.

TODAY I MOSTLY FELT:

DRAW HOW YOU FELT ON THE DRAGON'S FACE

DID ANYTHING MAKE ME FEEL ANXIOUS, FRUSTRATED OR SAD? IF SO, WHY?

_____
_____
_____
_____
_____

TOP THREE THINGS ABOUT TODAY:

(1) _____
(2) _____
(3) _____

THREE THINGS I'M GRATEFUL FOR TODAY:

(1) _____
(2) _____
(3) _____

M T W T F S S

DATE: _____

THREE THINGS I FELT TODAY:

1. _____
2. _____
3. _____

TODAY I MOSTLY FELT:

DRAW HOW YOU FELT ON THE DRAGON'S FACE

DID ANYTHING MAKE ME FEEL ANXIOUS, FRUSTRATED OR SAD? IF SO, WHY?

_____
_____
_____
_____
_____

TOP THREE THINGS ABOUT TODAY:

(1) _____
(2) _____
(3) _____

THREE THINGS I'M GRATEFUL FOR TODAY:

(1) _____
(2) _____
(3) _____

M T W T F S S

DATE: _____

THREE THINGS I FELT TODAY:

1. _____
2. _____
3. _____

TODAY I MOSTLY FELT:

DRAW HOW YOU FELT ON THE DRAGON'S FACE

DID ANYTHING MAKE ME FEEL ANXIOUS, FRUSTRATED OR SAD? IF SO, WHY?

_____
_____
_____
_____
_____

TOP THREE THINGS ABOUT TODAY:

(1) _____
(2) _____
(3) _____

THREE THINGS I'M GRATEFUL FOR TODAY:

(1) _____
(2) _____
(3) _____

M T W T F S S

DATE: _____

THREE THINGS I FELT TODAY:

1.
2.
3.

TODAY I MOSTLY FELT:

DRAW HOW YOU FELT ON THE DRAGON'S FACE

DID ANYTHING MAKE ME FEEL ANXIOUS, FRUSTRATED OR SAD? IF SO, WHY?

_____

_____

_____

_____

TOP THREE THINGS ABOUT TODAY:

(1) _____

(2) _____

(3) _____

THREE THINGS I'M GRATEFUL FOR TODAY:

(1) _____

(2) _____

(3) _____

THIS IS MY WORK OF ART

DATE: _____

DATE: _____

WRITE ABOUT A TIME YOU FELT NERVOUS OR ANXIOUS. WHAT HAPPENED?

_____

_____

_____

_____

_____

_____

_____

_____

_____

_____

_____

_____

_____

_____

_____

_____

_____

M T W T F S S

DATE: _____

THREE THINGS I FELT TODAY:

1.
2.
3.

TODAY I MOSTLY FELT:

DRAW HOW YOU FELT ON THE DRAGON'S FACE

DID ANYTHING MAKE ME FEEL ANXIOUS, FRUSTRATED OR SAD? IF SO, WHY?

_____

_____

_____

_____

_____

TOP THREE THINGS ABOUT TODAY:

① _____

② _____

③ _____

THREE THINGS I'M GRATEFUL FOR TODAY:

① _____

② _____

③ _____

M T W T F S S

DATE: _____

THREE THINGS I FELT TODAY:

1. _____
2. _____
3. _____

TODAY I MOSTLY FELT:

DRAW HOW YOU FELT ON THE DRAGON'S FACE

DID ANYTHING MAKE ME FEEL ANXIOUS, FRUSTRATED OR SAD? IF SO, WHY?

_____
_____
_____
_____

TOP THREE THINGS ABOUT TODAY:

1 _____
2 _____
3 _____

THREE THINGS I'M GRATEFUL FOR TODAY:

1 _____
2 _____
3 _____

M T W T F S S

DATE: _____

THREE THINGS I FELT TODAY:

1. _____
2. _____
3. _____

TODAY I MOSTLY FELT:

DRAW HOW YOU FELT ON THE DRAGON'S FACE

DID ANYTHING MAKE ME FEEL ANXIOUS, FRUSTRATED OR SAD? IF SO, WHY?

TOP THREE THINGS ABOUT TODAY:

1.
2.
3.

THREE THINGS I'M GRATEFUL FOR TODAY:

1.
2.
3.

M T W T F S S

DATE: _____

THREE THINGS I FELT TODAY:

1.
2.
3.

TODAY I MOSTLY FELT:

DRAW HOW YOU FELT ON THE DRAGON'S FACE

DID ANYTHING MAKE ME FEEL ANXIOUS, FRUSTRATED OR SAD? IF SO, WHY?

_____
_____
_____
_____
_____

TOP THREE THINGS ABOUT TODAY:

(1) _____
(2) _____
(3) _____

THREE THINGS I'M GRATEFUL FOR TODAY:

(1) _____
(2) _____
(3) _____

M T W T F S S

DATE: _____

THREE THINGS I FELT TODAY:

1. _____
2. _____
3. _____

TODAY I MOSTLY FELT:

DRAW HOW YOU FELT ON THE DRAGON'S FACE

DID ANYTHING MAKE ME FEEL ANXIOUS, FRUSTRATED OR SAD? IF SO, WHY?

_____
_____
_____
_____

TOP THREE THINGS ABOUT TODAY:

(1) _____
(2) _____
(3) _____

THREE THINGS I'M GRATEFUL FOR TODAY:

(1) _____
(2) _____
(3) _____

THIS IS MY WORK OF ART

DATE: _____

WRITE ABOUT A TIME SOMEONE MADE YOU FEEL GOOD ABOUT YOURSELF.

M T W T F S S

DATE: _____

THREE THINGS I FELT TODAY:

1
2
3

TODAY I MOSTLY FELT:

DRAW HOW YOU FELT ON THE DRAGON'S FACE

DID ANYTHING MAKE ME FEEL ANXIOUS, FRUSTRATED OR SAD? IF SO, WHY?

_____

_____

_____

_____

TOP THREE THINGS ABOUT TODAY:

1. _____

2. _____

3. _____

THREE THINGS I'M GRATEFUL FOR TODAY:

1. _____

2. _____

3. _____

M T W T F S S

DATE: _____

THREE THINGS I FELT TODAY:

1
2
3

TODAY I MOSTLY FELT:

DRAW HOW YOU FELT ON THE DRAGON'S FACE

DID ANYTHING MAKE ME FEEL ANXIOUS, FRUSTRATED OR SAD? IF SO, WHY?

_____
_____
_____
_____
_____

TOP THREE THINGS ABOUT TODAY:

1 _____
2 _____
3 _____

THREE THINGS I'M GRATEFUL FOR TODAY:

1 _____
2 _____
3 _____

M T W T F S S

DATE: _____

THREE THINGS I FELT TODAY:

1 _____
2 _____
3 _____

TODAY I MOSTLY FELT:

DRAW HOW YOU FELT ON THE DRAGON'S FACE

DID ANYTHING MAKE ME FEEL ANXIOUS, FRUSTRATED OR SAD? IF SO, WHY?

_____

_____

_____

_____

_____

TOP THREE THINGS ABOUT TODAY:

1 _____

2 _____

3 _____

THREE THINGS I'M GRATEFUL FOR TODAY:

1 _____

2 _____

3 _____

MTWTFSS

DATE: _____

THREE THINGS I FELT TODAY:

1. _____
2. _____
3. _____

TODAY I MOSTLY FELT:

DRAW HOW YOU FELT ON THE DRAGON'S FACE

DID ANYTHING MAKE ME FEEL ANXIOUS, FRUSTRATED OR SAD? IF SO, WHY?

TOP THREE THINGS ABOUT TODAY:

1.
2.
3.

THREE THINGS I'M GRATEFUL FOR TODAY:

1.
2.
3.

M T W T F S S

DATE: _____

THREE THINGS I FELT TODAY:

1. _____
2. _____
3. _____

TODAY I MOSTLY FELT:

DRAW HOW YOU FELT ON THE DRAGON'S FACE

DID ANYTHING MAKE ME FEEL ANXIOUS, FRUSTRATED OR SAD? IF SO, WHY?

TOP THREE THINGS ABOUT TODAY:

1
2
3

THREE THINGS I'M GRATEFUL FOR TODAY:

1
2
3

THIS IS MY WORK OF ART

DATE: _____

DATE: _____

WHAT DOES IT MEAN TO BE A GOOD FRIEND?

_____

_____

_____

_____

_____

_____

_____

_____

_____

_____

_____

_____

_____

_____

_____

_____

M T W T F S S

DATE: _____

THREE THINGS I FELT TODAY:

1 _____
2 _____
3 _____

TODAY I MOSTLY FELT:

DRAW HOW YOU FELT ON THE DRAGON'S FACE

DID ANYTHING MAKE ME FEEL ANXIOUS, FRUSTRATED OR SAD? IF SO, WHY?

_____

_____

_____

_____

TOP THREE THINGS ABOUT TODAY:

1. _____
2. _____
3. _____

THREE THINGS I'M GRATEFUL FOR TODAY:

1. _____
2. _____
3. _____

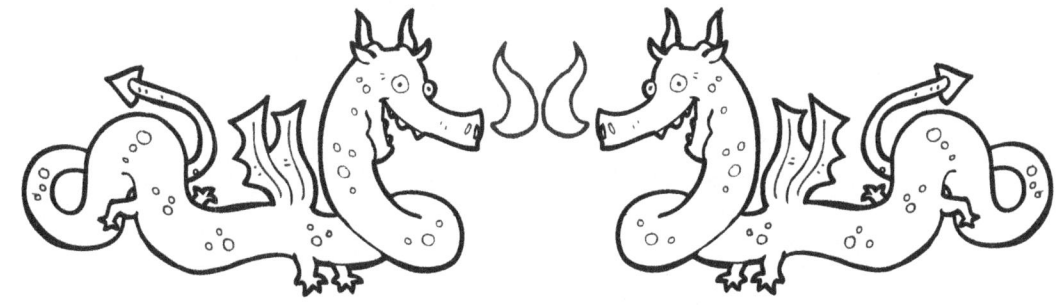

MTWTFSS

DATE: _____

THREE THINGS I FELT TODAY:

1
2
3

TODAY I MOSTLY FELT:

DRAW HOW YOU FELT ON THE DRAGON'S FACE

DID ANYTHING MAKE ME FEEL ANXIOUS, FRUSTRATED OR SAD? IF SO, WHY?

_____
_____
_____
_____
_____

TOP THREE THINGS ABOUT TODAY:

(1) _____
(2) _____
(3) _____

THREE THINGS I'M GRATEFUL FOR TODAY:

(1) _____
(2) _____
(3) _____

M T W T F S S

DATE: _____

THREE THINGS I FELT TODAY:

1.
2.
3.

TODAY I MOSTLY FELT:

DRAW HOW YOU FELT ON THE DRAGON'S FACE

DID ANYTHING MAKE ME FEEL ANXIOUS, FRUSTRATED OR SAD? IF SO, WHY?

_____

_____

_____

_____

TOP THREE THINGS ABOUT TODAY:

1 _____

2 _____

3 _____

THREE THINGS I'M GRATEFUL FOR TODAY:

1 _____

2 _____

3 _____

M T W T F S S

DATE: _____

THREE THINGS I FELT TODAY:

1. Excited
2. happiness
3. impatience

TODAY I MOSTLY FELT:

DRAW HOW YOU FELT ON THE DRAGON'S FACE

DID ANYTHING MAKE ME FEEL ANXIOUS, FRUSTRATED OR SAD? IF SO, WHY?

I did not feel any of this because I am going to oman.

TOP THREE THINGS ABOUT TODAY:

1. going to oman
2. meeting Mohammed
3. give mustu mamu his gift

THREE THINGS I'M GRATEFUL FOR TODAY:

1. going to oman
2. going to matbnasian
3. mom bing nice

M T W T F S S

DATE: _____

THREE THINGS I FELT TODAY:

1.
2.
3.

TODAY I MOSTLY FELT:

DRAW HOW YOU FELT ON THE DRAGON'S FACE

DID ANYTHING MAKE ME FEEL ANXIOUS, FRUSTRATED OR SAD? IF SO, WHY?

TOP THREE THINGS ABOUT TODAY:

1
2
3

THREE THINGS I'M GRATEFUL FOR TODAY:

1
2
3

THIS IS MY WORK OF ART

DATE: _____

DATE: _____

WHAT AGE ARE YOU MOST LOOKING FORWARD TO IN THE FUTURE?

_____

_____

_____

_____

_____

_____

_____

_____

_____

_____

_____

_____

_____

_____

_____

_____

_____

M T W T F S S

DATE: _____

THREE THINGS I FELT TODAY:

1. _____
2. _____
3. _____

TODAY I MOSTLY FELT:

DRAW HOW YOU FELT ON THE DRAGON'S FACE

DID ANYTHING MAKE ME FEEL ANXIOUS, FRUSTRATED OR SAD? IF SO, WHY?

_____

_____

_____

_____

_____

TOP THREE THINGS ABOUT TODAY:

(1) _____

(2) _____

(3) _____

THREE THINGS I'M GRATEFUL FOR TODAY:

(1) _____

(2) _____

(3) _____

MTWTFSS

DATE: _____

THREE THINGS I FELT TODAY:

1.
2.
3.

TODAY I MOSTLY FELT:

DRAW HOW YOU FELT ON THE DRAGON'S FACE

DID ANYTHING MAKE ME FEEL ANXIOUS, FRUSTRATED OR SAD? IF SO, WHY?

_____
_____
_____
_____

TOP THREE THINGS ABOUT TODAY:

① _____
② _____
③ _____

THREE THINGS I'M GRATEFUL FOR TODAY:

① _____
② _____
③ _____

M T W T F S S

DATE: _____

THREE THINGS I FELT TODAY:

 ① _____
 ② _____
 ③ _____

TODAY I MOSTLY FELT:

😀 🙂

☹️ 😠

😢 😬

DRAW HOW YOU FELT ON THE DRAGON'S FACE

DID ANYTHING MAKE ME FEEL ANXIOUS, FRUSTRATED OR SAD? IF SO, WHY?

TOP THREE THINGS ABOUT TODAY:

1.
2.
3.

THREE THINGS I'M GRATEFUL FOR TODAY:

1.
2.
3.

M T W T F S S

DATE: _____

THREE THINGS I FELT TODAY:

1. _____
2. _____
3. _____

TODAY I MOSTLY FELT:

DRAW HOW YOU FELT ON THE DRAGON'S FACE

DID ANYTHING MAKE ME FEEL ANXIOUS, FRUSTRATED OR SAD? IF SO, WHY?

_____

_____

_____

_____

_____

TOP THREE THINGS ABOUT TODAY:

1 _____

2 _____

3 _____

THREE THINGS I'M GRATEFUL FOR TODAY:

1 _____

2 _____

3 _____

M T W T F S S

DATE: _____

THREE THINGS I FELT TODAY:

1. _____
2. _____
3. _____

TODAY I MOSTLY FELT:

DRAW HOW YOU FELT ON THE DRAGON'S FACE

DID ANYTHING MAKE ME FEEL ANXIOUS, FRUSTRATED OR SAD? IF SO, WHY?

TOP THREE THINGS ABOUT TODAY:

1.
2.
3.

THREE THINGS I'M GRATEFUL FOR TODAY:

1.
2.
3.

THIS IS MY WORK OF ART

DATE:

Respect

WHAT IS THE MOST INTERESTING THING YOU'VE DONE?

The most intresting Thing I have done was playing a soccer match. In the Inteting start any team was wining by 4-0. In mid game the counter team somehow got in Insaoly ber beter the scor was than 2-1 they were wining we tryd are best thoug I mang to secor at the best gouly and get the ball from the best player pranes. Althou we didn't win we came close and a scor of 5-7. It was a very fun game.

M T W T F S S

DATE: _____

THREE THINGS I FELT TODAY:

① _____
② _____
③ _____

TODAY I MOSTLY FELT:

DRAW HOW YOU FELT ON THE DRAGON'S FACE

DID ANYTHING MAKE ME FEEL ANXIOUS, FRUSTRATED OR SAD? IF SO, WHY?

TOP THREE THINGS ABOUT TODAY:

1
2
3

THREE THINGS I'M GRATEFUL FOR TODAY:

1
2
3

M T W T F S S

DATE: _____

THREE THINGS I FELT TODAY:

1 _____
2 _____
3 _____

TODAY I MOSTLY FELT:

DRAW HOW YOU FELT ON THE DRAGON'S FACE

DID ANYTHING MAKE ME FEEL ANXIOUS, FRUSTRATED OR SAD? IF SO, WHY?

TOP THREE THINGS ABOUT TODAY:

1.
2.
3.

THREE THINGS I'M GRATEFUL FOR TODAY:

1.
2.
3.

M T W T F S S

DATE: _____

THREE THINGS I FELT TODAY:

1. _____
2. _____
3. _____

TODAY I MOSTLY FELT:

DRAW HOW YOU FELT ON THE DRAGON'S FACE

DID ANYTHING MAKE ME FEEL ANXIOUS, FRUSTRATED OR SAD? IF SO, WHY?

_____
_____
_____
_____
_____

TOP THREE THINGS ABOUT TODAY:

(1) _____
(2) _____
(3) _____

THREE THINGS I'M GRATEFUL FOR TODAY:

(1) _____
(2) _____
(3) _____

M T W T F S S

DATE: _____

THREE THINGS I FELT TODAY:

1.
2.
3.

TODAY I MOSTLY FELT:

DRAW HOW YOU FELT ON THE DRAGON'S FACE

DID ANYTHING MAKE ME FEEL ANXIOUS, FRUSTRATED OR SAD? IF SO, WHY?

_____

_____

_____

_____

TOP THREE THINGS ABOUT TODAY:

(1) _____

(2) _____

(3) _____

THREE THINGS I'M GRATEFUL FOR TODAY:

(1) _____

(2) _____

(3) _____

THIS IS MY WORK OF ART

DATE: _____

DATE: _____

IF YOU COULD BE A SUPERHERO WHAT SPECIAL POWERS WOULD YOU CHOOSE?

_____

_____

_____

_____

_____

_____

_____

_____

_____

_____

_____

_____

_____

_____

_____

_____

If you like this book, please give us a positive rating and review on Amazon - it means a lot! Scan below to go to the book review page.

Excited

Made in the USA
Monee, IL
10 March 2023

29582205R00063